why wear those
Hoochie Mama
dresses?

WHAT'S YOUR STYLE—ROYALTY OR RISQUÉ?

Martha **Cahoon**

TATE PUBLISHING, LLC

ISBN: 1–5988620–8-1

Dedication

To my husband, an example of the man Peter,
who stood by the fire of denial and testing
and came away from it a better man.

Thank you, my encourager, my soul
mate, my friend . . . Mike.

Acknowledgements

To my precious daughters who encouraged
and supported my vision in writing this book.
Paige, who continued to remind me of the need.
Angie, who kept telling me I could do it.
Michelle, my daughter-in-law,
who inspired the title.
Also to my son, Kelly, who reminded me that
with my mind, I should keep this book short.
To friends who gave the help
of their computer skills.

Table of Contents

Foreword

As a father of a beautiful five-year-old daughter, I am often stunned, alarmed and amazed at the amount of pressure society has placed on women, especially young women, to flaunt their sexuality. There are so many voices in our culture that are calling out and receiving the attention of our daughters. From Jessica Simpson to Madonna to 50 Cent the message to young ladies is your value is found in your sexuality and sexual expression through dress. Many of these voices have confused lust with love, perversion with purity, eroticism with intimacy.

In a culture that has lost its way concerning purity, Martha Cahoon comes as a clarion voice of one crying in this wilderness. Her message is clear. Your value as a lady is found in the fact that you were created in the likeness and the image of God. You are a princess–a daughter of the King Eternal. You are accepted! You are uniquely beautiful! You are special to the King and His Kingdom. He clothes you in His righteousness,

His love, and His mercy and even sings a song of love over you (Zephaniah 3:17). However, this does not suggest that a lady whose heart follows passionately after her King must abandon all fashion sense and fill her closet with gunnysacks and period clothing from the 1600's. On the contrary, this young lady recognizes her inner beauty and then compliments such beauty with 'fine linens' that reflect her creativity, fashion sense and testimony of a life lived for the King.

"Why Wear Those Hoochie Mama Dresses" is going to encourage you, make you laugh and cause you to honestly examine your fashion choices. If you are a parent, I pray that as you read this book, that the Father will encourage you to engage your daughter in open and honest conversation; helping her to see her remarkable value and beauty. If you are a young lady, I pray as you read this book that your heart will be pliable and open to the voice of your loving Heavenly Father, that you will see how beautifully he has made you and the beauty that comes from being clothed in His glory.

Rev. Tony Vismor
Senior Pastor
Grace Fellowship

Introduction

A trip to the mall is not what it used to be. Gone are the exciting mother and daughter marathon shopping trips to drool over beautiful fashions while looking for the perfect dream garment. The success of the trip was marked by finding the garment for a steal of a price while the body reached exhilarating exhaustion.

Those days have been replaced by stress, disagreement, temper tantrums, and down-right dressing room brawls. Why? Women's clothing is not what it used to be. Fashions are dictating that innocence and purity be exploited by wearing clothing that looks as if it came from a mall in Sodom and Gomorrah. On the other hand, mom, whose instincts are in protection mode, is desperately looking for a mall on an exit off the yellow brick road. So today this is what many shopping trips look like: Stressed out mothers, anxious to protect their daughter's modesty, points out clothing that they feel is appropriate. The daughter, appalled by the lack of creativity, objects. This in turn leads to disagreement, which eventually results in a temper tantrum, which explodes in the dressing room with a verbal brawl as mom and daughter both shout long and hard, "No!"

Being a mother of two daughters, I have fought the battles in the mall dressing rooms, so I can identify with most mothers experiencing the same problem. But also, as a young teenager, I designed and made most of my own clothing because I enjoyed creative and unique fashions. So I identify with young creative girls and women who enjoy these styles. From this background comes my vantage point in writing this book. However, my perspective is influenced completely by my understanding and obedience to the Bible and what God says about the clothing we place upon our bodies.

Why Wear Those Hoochie Mama Dresses is not a book of compromise; it is a book that enables the reader to move toward self-examination. In a day when family unity and morality are being threatened on every front, the world of fashion is one that has been blatantly tolerated as a menacing harm. This book is blended with light humor and whimsy, and has a balance between what the fashionably dressed woman desires in a garment and what the Bible requires for holiness.

chapter 1

Where is "You Go Girl" Going?

"The dress you wore to the wedding was beautiful, Michelle, and it fit perfectly!"

My young daughter-in-law and I were visiting a few minutes with a cup of coffee at my breakfast table. The topic of conversation was the wedding she had recently attended.

"You really liked it?" Her eyebrows arched high over her pale blue eyes.

"It was made for you," I said. "The scooped neckline and the dropped waist looked great, and the black damask fabric was so chic."

"I liked it, too," she replied, "but after I got to the wedding I felt a little fashion intimidated."

"Why in the world would you be intimidated as pretty as you looked?" I asked as I took a long sip of hot coffee.

"Well, you know," Michelle hesitated briefly, "I looked a little modest compared to all those girls in their hoochie mama dresses."

I spewed my coffee across the table, surprised at the words that came out of her mouth. "Hoochie mama dresses!" I shrieked in my most distressed southern drawl. "Michelle, what in the world are hoochie mama dresses?"

"Well, you've seen them before," she said as she carefully wrapped both hands around her coffee mug. Then in her sultriest southern drawl continued, "They are cut low to show mo' and hemmed high to show thigh."

I got the picture completely.

The topic of mine and Michelle's conversation is one that brings giggles, elbow nudges, and cheers like, "You go, girl." But this topic is being lived out among girls and women alike today because "You go, girl" is going farther beyond the fashion and moral lines than she has ever gone before.

"So it's a free country," we say, "every woman should have the freedom to exercise her personal clothing taste." And then we add quickly with moral tongue in cheek, "As long as no one is harmed by our preference, who cares?"

However, perhaps we should consider the possibility of harm to ourselves and to others as a result of our clothing preference. And if there is possibility of harm–what responsibility do we assume? And how will the harm affect us today or possibly into the future? I know these questions sound like ones asked to the ten finalists in the Miss America Pageant (and the answer could be world peace), but don't skip over to the middle of this book yet. The worst scenario I can think of is this book laying in the bottom of a trashcan or on your coffee table with dust on it. So I am going straight to the point and then we will move on to more stimulating reading.

chapter 2

You Talkin' to Me?

Girls, the secret is out. The whole world knows—women have the power of influence. A woman is a natural mentor and nurturer; instinct nudges her to foster nourishment and guidance to those around her. Since the beginning of time women as wives, mothers, sisters, friends and advisors, have perpetually made an impact in their sphere of influence. This includes the childhood years spent playing with other children in the sandbox to the adulthood years where we learn to use life's responsibilities and opportunities to influence others. It is not difficult to realize that because of a woman's natural position as an influencer and mentor that—as a woman goes, so might a country.

So does it make sense that the downhill slide in a country's morals is in part due to the woman compromising moral values? The compromise may result from poor choices, sexual indiscretions, low standards and expectations of her life and, yes, even clothing preference. And when we look at the full picture, it is not difficult to understand how this can happen. Mankind, culture, and natural desires constantly chip against the wall of a woman's resistance, wearing down her will to do the more excellent thing. In herself, the responsibility and pressure are enormous, but nevertheless, as the advances of immorality creep forward, it's the woman who must draw the line in society's sand. And this is true with women of all ages, from the teenage girl to the mature woman as well.

"Well do tell, how has this responsibility fallen on the woman's shoulder?" we ask. "And how does clothing preference fit into all of this?" We toss back our hair, jab our hands on our hips, and nod our head from side to side in beat with each word of the question. And the answer to the question is clear–because women have the power of influence. Not only do we influence in our verbal presence, body language, and moral character, but in the signals our clothing sends out as well. A woman, whether she realizes it or not, is an ever present spur in the life of any number of individuals. So it is no difficult matter to understand that a woman's power of influence can gradually eat away the character and integrity of those around her or it can have a positive effect and build it up.

Okay, girls, I know what our reaction is at this point. We blow air in our hair and stomp off to a land called I DON'T EVEN WANT TO HEAR THIS. Then we quickly ask in our defense, "Well, which women are we to blame anyway?" This is a very good question. Do we blame our great grandmothers with ruffles on all three layers of their underwear or the new generation with holes in the seats of their jeans where there appears to be no underwear at all? Will a poll on the street find that the older woman blames the younger woman and the younger woman blames the older?

Seriously, we don't have time for blame. Let's forget the past and look forward to what we can do with the future. Rather than blame, let's

martha cahoon

see how each generation can help the other. And perhaps we should learn an ancient practice of "pondering" and think on all of this a bit.

martha cahoon

chapter 3

Older Women Teach What is Good!

"Older women are to teach what is
good and to teach the young women to
be sensible and pure."
Titus 2:3 (TLB)

The answer to all of life is found in the
Bible. When we read the scriptures we see that
a moral problem is actually a spiritual problem.
The book of Titus, found in the New Testament
of the Bible, shows us a starting place that can
make a difference in the moral healing of our
lives. Chapter two in Titus says, "Older women
are to teach what is good and to teach the young
women to be sensible and pure."

According to this scripture it appears that

older women have work cut out for themselves. But older women should understand, they cannot take anyone farther morally or spiritually than they have gone themselves. Perhaps that sentence states a part of the purpose and passion for writing this book. The average woman today, young and old, is more educated and better equipped intellectually, is financially more stable, healthier, lives longer and has many more years to enjoy retirement than earlier generations. What an impact today's woman could make in our world if she were prepared to mentor young girls and women. Not to suggest that the mentor must be older than the individual she is mentoring. Wisdom is not always measured in an individual's physical years. It is measured in knowledge, experience, spiritual understanding, and most importantly, how we have allowed these properties to influence our lives. I have seen teenage girls teach and mentor women old enough to be their mothers. How? Because the teenager is more spiritually mature and it results in wisdom and understanding.

However, there is a primary area this book wishes to target, and that is in the area of women's fashions. This is obviously an area that is in our face constantly, but never seriously addressed because there are always too many more pressing problems in our society. Who has time to address the hem length going up when the crime rate is up by figures large enough to stagger us? But if clothing designs were examined in relation to a number of society's problems, we may find there is reason to believe that sensual dress is a partial contributor to the problem.

For instance, let's take the rape crime problem. A National Crime Victimization Survey through the Bureau of Justice Statistics in 2000 will show that there are 1.3 women raped every minute in the United States.[1] That is 683,280 rapes committed each year. Rape is the fastest growing crime in the United States. Please understand that by no means are all rapes committed because a woman has carelessly dressed herself. This violent crime attacks women whose lives are exemplary of innocence and good character. But for sake of example, ponder on this bit of simple but interesting information. Studies have shown that the number of rape cases go up in proportion to the amount of ice cream sold in

---

[1] http://bjsdata.ojp.usdoj.gov/dataonline/Search/Crime/State/

martha cahoon

our country. Why? Because ice cream sales go up in the summer months, when girls are more often wearing scantily attired clothing.

I am not suggesting that the complexity of the rape crime problem can be solved by closing down ice cream parlors. But I am suggesting that our clothing styles are stimuli to some of the moral problems within our troubled society. Which reminds me, I did promise more stimulating reading after we got through this introduction. Well, let's move on, then.

martha cahoon

chapter 4

Sssso, There's a Ssssnake in the Camp

"But I am frightened, fearing that in some way you will be led away from your pure and simple devotion to our Lord, just as Eve was deceived by Satan in the garden."

II Corinthians 11:3 (TLB)

There is much concern today about the difficulty of girls preserving their purity in a world that is out of control sexually. Parents are looking for solutions by rating movies, placing age control on buying alcohol and strong vigilance on drug control. Many families are moving to safer neighborhoods, transferring children to private schools, and finding a church with well staffed youth and children's groups. And all of these are good and positive actions that help set up guards against premarital sex for young daughters and sons.

But girls today do not necessarily lose their innocence or purity in sexual promiscuity. Our daughters lose their purity when they begin compromising themselves in the manner in which they dress. Their desire to look like the rest of the world is a slow, downhill decline morally that in their minds is justified with the exclamation, "But everybody's wearing it!"

Most every female has a strong and tempting desire to look like her peers and to be accepted by them. But even this is not the real root of the problem. You see, the one who tempts us girls is the old serpent that twisted his way into the Garden of Eden and tempted the first woman, Eve. Let it be understood, that snake was the best dressed piece of flesh that ever slithered onto Main Street, Eden. Eve took one look at his beautiful skin and began to believe everything he said, not to mention how great a pair of shoes would look made out of his hide (and she had never worn shoes before).

But hold on a minute! Who is this serpent? Is he real? Perhaps you are thinking, I don't have to worry about this snake. I don't even have a garden. I am surrounded by miles of hot concrete, too hot for slithering. And these days there is a snake-eating, salivating Rottweiler dog on every other block.

But according to the Bible we should be aware that the enemy is a DECEIVER (II Corinthians 11:3). He can slither along the grassy cracks in the hot concrete and charm his way past the mouth-slobbering Rottweilers to lead us astray from our pure and simple devotion to Christ.

Perhaps you ask, "What is pure and simple devotion to Christ? And what is the deal with this snake anyway? Isn't this all a bit antiquated and unrealistic? After all, we live in a complicated world so nothing is simple. Purity no longer exists and most snakes are on the endangered species list." Suppose we take this subject slow and easy and answer one question at a time.

Question One: "What is pure and simple

martha cahoon

devotion to Christ?" Every person that has a relationship with Christ will respond to a different level in their devotion to Him. The reason being is that every person who believes in Jesus Christ is at a different level of growth and commitment in their spiritual walk. But if we are serious about a pure relationship with Him, we will constantly be placing that relationship beside a true standard. That standard is God's Word and it is written, "For you have been bought with a price. Therefore, glorify God in your body." (I Corinthians 6:20)

When we truly grasp the great price paid for each of our lives by the death of Jesus Christ for our sins, then pure and simple devotion to Christ will be the most important thing in our lives, in every area of our lives, including our wardrobes. Perhaps you doubt, wondering if it is possible to come to this depth of relationship with God. Jeremiah 29:13 tells us how to reach this depth, "And you will seek Me and find Me when you search for Me with all your heart." So it is possible.

I realize there may be some readers who have absolutely no relationship with Jesus Christ and you are ready to throw this book to the Rottweilers. Just keep on reading. What I have to say is at least entertaining, so this will not be a complete waste of time.

Question Two: "Who is this snake?" According to the scriptures we see him emerge in Genesis 3:1, which says, "The serpent was the CRAFTIEST of all the creatures the Lord God had made." (TLB) This serpent is the devil, our enemy, and he is seen at work throughout the Bible. His job description is found in the New Testament in John 10:10, which describes him as a thief and it says, "The thief's purpose is to steal, kill, and destroy." (TLB) Sounds like a modern day terminator, doesn't he? He is–but with more experience, more ammunition, more camouflage, and he is more deadly than anything we have ever encountered. A little research on Satan will disclose the fact that he at one time was one of God's angels. His name was Lucifer. He was handsome and his clothing was made with beautiful jewels. He was also the angel who made the music for the worship of God. But he became so prideful of his appearance, clothing, and talents that he desired to raise himself above God. So God cast him out of heaven (Ezekiel 28). Here on

martha cahoon

earth he "prowls about like a roaring lion, seeking someone to devour." (I Peter 5:8).

But heads up! The remainder of John 10:10 is much more exciting because it gives Jesus' job description. It says, "My purpose is to give life in all its fullness." (TLB) this is the opposite of the terminator. Jesus is the life giver. He desires that each of us experience His best for our lives. "For I know the plans that I have for you," declares the Lord, "plans for welfare and not for calamity, to give you a future and a hope." (Jeremiah 29:11).

Then why is it so difficult to decide whom we will follow with resumes so graphic? Remember in Genesis 3:1 it says the serpent is the CRAFTIEST of all the creatures? That is exactly what he is. By craftiness and deception, he will pervert what God intended to give our lives fullness. The devil will kill our purity, steal our dreams, and destroy our future. He will accomplish this by tiny, little baby steps and with steady progression lead us into situations of greater and greater compromise. The style of clothing we put on our bodies each day can be part of the compromise.

Hold on! Before you bounce off the wall in a panic, running for the nearest closet to find a place to hide–this is not a Girl Scout camping trip, sitting in the dark around a bonfire, telling the scariest story kind of book. This is real life and there is a way to equip ourselves against this evil threat. But before we get into the solution, let's look at the problem, which brings us back to the subject of clothing and style and that snake we are going to get rid of soon.

chapter 5

Sssso You Want to Be in Sssstyle

"And Esther found favor in the eyes
of all who saw her."

Esther 2:15

Women like pretty clothing. They are born
that way. That's why baby girls cry when they are
born. They are screaming, "Put a pink ribbon in
my hair!" Baby boys cry because they hear baby
girls crying. Remember the power of influence?

The fact that we like pretty clothing can be
traced to our genes. And not only traced to our
genes, but in our jeans because over-tight jeans
keep the sexual revolution alive. Don't get me
wrong, I am the queen of jeans, and there are

37

several pairs in my closet. But Satan says keep the sssslack out of jeans, so many women walk around like they are sssssprayed on.

Seriously, God placed within us girls the desire to be pretty and to groom and pamper ourselves. In fact, there are several Godly women in the Bible that reflect these characteristics and it's worth our time to check them out.

There is one entire book written about a woman named Esther. Esther was a young, beautiful, and devout Jewish maiden that God used to rescue His people. We read where she won the favor of many in the king's court and was given special use of bath oils, perfumes, jewelry, and clothing. As a result, we see that she became the choice of the king and he loved Esther more than any of the other young women. He was so delighted with her that he set the royal crown on her head and declared her to be queen.

I will be quick to mention that Esther's life also reflected Godly traits such as wisdom, discernment, and integrity which won her favor as well. She had that "pure and simple devotion to God" that we read about earlier. But her natural feminine instincts to tastefully groom and adorn herself for the glory of God certainly got her a foot in the door. The scripture says, "And Esther found favor in the eyes of all who saw her."

This is a wonderful true story about this young woman. However, we should keep in mind what God created for good, Satan wants to pervert and destroy (remember John 10:10). Here on earth he works to destroy purity and innocence by replacing them with cheap substitutes. He knows that girls like pretty clothing and that we want to be stylish and accepted by our peers. So Satan takes advantage of opportunity made available through the fashion industry to make a tremendous impact on our lives without our realizing the underlying motive. "How so?" we ask. Because girls want to look nice, not only for themselves, but for the opposite sex as well. This again is normal. God designed us that way. Now, note that the fashion designers are in the business to make money, so designs are created that will appeal to the natural desires of men. Satan subtly impresses upon women that the more provocatively we dress, the more likely we are to attract men. And we do, but for the wrong reasons. So women keep buying and the fashion industry keeps cranking out the designs that women are looking for, with the clothing becoming more and more risqué each year.

Understand, we cannot lay all of the fault with the fashion designers. We should be aware that our society is raising up a generation of young men that cannot be satisfied sexually. Because their eyes, ears, and minds have been bombarded all their lives with sexuality on television, in the movie theaters, music, and online pornography, their sexual appetites are unrealistic and out of control. As a result, young women are being pressured to compete with the media sources, so we compromise all modesty in our dress in order to stimulate this man's attention and approval. But understand, a woman's efforts will never measure up or be enough to satisfy him. This new generation young man expects to see greater levels of seduction than he has already experienced and his expectation will always be raising the bar higher on sexual satisfaction.

Beware young girls and women, this is a lose/lose situation. It is not a time to have a blond (brunette or red head) moment. This is a time when we should be walking in wisdom and understanding of possible consequences. Proverbs 3:13–15 tells us in the Message Bible, "You're blessed when you meet Lady Wisdom, when you make friends with Madame Insight. She's worth far more than money in the bank; her friendship is better than a big salary. Her value exceeds all the trappings of wealth, nothing you could wish for holds a candle to her."

With this scripture in mind, I believe that in order to add more quality to our lives we should become wise rather than become a fool (definition of a fool in Webster is nincompoop or brainless). Yes, the word fool is a four letter word, and we need to know there are consequences for becoming one. Also, another word for you is Charlatan. This is someone that would ask a woman to compromise her body for their amusement (definition of Charlatan in Webster is a cheat, faker, *quack*). Don't become a Charlatan's blond (brunette or red head) Monday morning joke. Charlatans' have been around since the Garden of Eden, but each generation gives them a different name. Just know that the application of godly wisdom will ALWAYS add greater value in your life and will keep you from acting like a brainless nincom-

martha cahoon

poop and being taken advantage of by a cheat
and a faker that sounds like a duck!

martha cahoon

chapter 6

But Everybody's Wearing Them!

"As a ring of gold in a swine's snout, so is a beautiful woman who lacks discretion."

Proverbs 11:22

But everybody's wearing them! Yes, they are. Young girls see the clothing at every advertising and promotional opportunity that the fashion world offers. They see the young female vocalist appearing on television. She skips around on stage singing her heart out, wearing a new fashion statement that leaves very little to the imagination there is so much flesh exposed. One would think the music was coming out of her bosom or belly button with so much attention being placed there.

Then there are the magazine ads that are filled with young women wearing the latest trend. As the young models pose, wearing the new fashions, their bodies send off an attitude of seduction and sensuality, giving a message that this is a byproduct of wearing the garment. The public falls for the bait, purchases the designs, and soon the clothing hits the street. It will now be seen everywhere from the classroom to the uniform on the cherub-faced cheerleader. The designs then work their way to the housewife pushing the grocery cart down the supermarket aisle. And a short while later, they are seen in the workplace worn by women working in offices, schools, fast food restaurants, retail establishments, and so on.

Eventually the clothing appears in the last place on earth you would expect–in the church. Shocked, we ask, "How can this be?" It happens because Christian women also want to be in style and for the sake of fashion and flesh, we compromise. So we decide to wear our wardrobes to worship, and arm in arm, Satan and style walk through the door, and you will notice Satan has on those snakeskin shoes.

martha cahoon

The enemy wins prized territory when he brings distraction into God's house. Remember his job description? He comes to steal, kill, and destroy, and if he can keep our minds and eyes from being Christ focused, he will steal the worship God has for us in His house.

An example of this happened in a church I visited recently. During the Sunday morning worship service, the children were having a special music presentation. Their excited little energetic bodies were lined in rows in front of the church altar facing the congregation. A young woman directing the music was standing in front of the children with her back to the congregation. The first song the children sang was entitled, "Be careful, little eyes, what you see."

The young woman leading the children raised her arms to direct the music and her chicly tailored miniskirt came up as well and stopped just below the control top in her pantyhose. It was amazing grace that kept her derriere from shining.

The children completed the first verse and continued singing the next line of the chorus, "Be careful, little hands, what you touch. Be care-

martha cahoon

ful little hands what you touch, be careful little hands, be careful little hands, be careful little hands what you touch." Their little round mouths sang the words in cherub-like innocence as the verse went on and on. At this point, the words of the song and the minds of the congregation were in sync. The director continued to wave her arms in the air urging the best out of the little choir while her nearly exposed booty accentuated the tempo of the music. I do not believe a spiritual thought was conceived by the congregation during the remainder of the service.

Are we thinking that our society should establish Clothing Cops and begin arresting women, placing them in the Wardrobe Abuse Clinic for the addiction to hoochie mama dressing? Nope, it would never work. It would be just another program to place the responsibility on someone else. Of course, this is a preposterous suggestion, not intentionally belittling the law enforcement of our country. And may we never forget this is a wonderful country we live in, our freedoms earned by the precious spilled blood of our countrymen. So as women, we should hold dear the responsibility of fighting to preserve our country's moral fiber and consider the influence that our clothing preference has upon its moral character.

Earlier we read the statistics on rape in the United States. There are other sexually related statistics that are also a reflection of declining morals that could be noted as well. Statistics such as the number of teenagers that have pre-marital sex, the number of abortions, the number of unwed mothers, and the number of young men and women with sexually transmitted diseases. Seeing the nature of these statistics and the opportunity for clothing choices to factor into an individual's decision making during a moment of infatuation, does this again raise the question, "Could our clothing choices have some degree of influence upon moral decisions?"

chapter 7

Understanding the Bare Facts

"As the deer pants for the water brook, so my soul pants for thee, O God."

Psalms 42:1

The most enchanting years of a girl's life are the years they anticipate the discovery of the man with whom they will live the rest of their lives. This is another natural desire that God placed within us girls and when we glorify God as we respond to that desire, it is an exciting time in our lives. But beware:our skills need to be fine tuned in godliness, careful grooming, and subtleness. If each one of these skills is kept in proper perspective, the man will never know he was not the hunter.

To illustrate a point, let us go back in time and stop just before processed meat. That would be when men had to go out into the wilds and track and kill game so they could eat. It was their work, not their recreation at that time, so it was not supposed to be any fun. It was a time when they had to survive by the male instincts that God had placed within them.

Let's say during this period of history a man goes hunting to find food. As he moves quietly through the woods, a deer foolishly walks into a clearing and deliberately exposes her presence. Not only does this doe expose her presence, but she carelessly remains in the open not bothering to find covering. The deer may or may not be aware that she is flirting with danger, but nevertheless she acts with reckless abandon and may likely pay the consequences. The hunter, not believing his good luck, takes careful aim and shoots the deer and then says, "Easy meal." Soon after this adventure is over, he quickly forgets about the conquest because the hunt was so unchallenging.

Then on another day, this same hunter goes

into the woods to hunt and he sees glimpses of another deer. This doe is smart and she stays elusive and covered by the forest around her. The man sees only bits and pieces of her, but the little he sees motivates his pursuit. He is intrigued by her mystique and traces her trail in the woods and undergrowth. The hunter studies her habits and is impressed by her skill at survival. He begins to respect her savvy and cunning. And all the while he is pursuing and studying her, he is in no hurry to rush the hunt because he realizes he has found a prized trophy.

The point is, a man is turned on by sight, but may soon lose interest after he has seen it all because there is nothing left to intrigue his imagination. But on the other hand, a man's curiosity is stimulated by what he can't see, so he will take greater detail in the chase, thus giving him time to develop a relationship in the pursuit.

This type of relationship is difficult today because the clothing styles are so brief that they leave very little to a young man's imagination. With more and more flesh exposed and body parts accentuated, men are invited to see it all; consequently, many relationships are brief, shallow conquests and the male moves on.

All the laws in our country, private schools, church youth groups, and camps in the world cannot protect our daughters or our young sons from being seduced if girls walk around with skirts just below hiney level and sweaters so tight they reveal every seam in the undergarment or the absence of an undergarment. Today's girls and women are dressing more and more like prostitutes and less and less with feminine quality. Then they react offended when disrespect is paid their demeanor. Is there any wonder that men are echoing in loud resound, "If you are not for sale, please take the sign down!"

I am reminded of a beautiful young college girl who walked down the aisle of a large church on an early Sunday morning. The sunlight shining through the arched windows fell softly on her hair and pretty face. She was a striking beauty and I watched her as she walked to the front of the crowded church to find a seat. She was wearing a very short, tight, silk dress with spaghetti straps that looked a twin sister to a slip. A woman seated in front of me saw her as well. She leaned toward her husband seated beside her and whispered, "Scott, do you think that young woman forget to put on another item of clothing this morning before leaving home?" Scott, with eyes wide in observation and a sly grin on his face answered, "Well, if it was a cap I don't think anyone has noticed."

Finally the young woman found her seat, but not before every male eye in the congregation had her zeroed into target. She reminded me of the deer that walked carelessly into the clearing.

It is no compliment to a woman when a man gawks at her because she publicly seduces him by immodest clothing selections. But it is a compliment when a man admiringly glances at her when she is modestly and attractively attired. To place doubt on the integrity of a woman's character is usually the result of seductive dressing. The Message Youth Bible says it non to gently in its paraphrase when it reads, "Like a gold ring in a pig's snout is a beautiful face on an empty head." (Proverbs 11:22)

Ouch!

martha cahoon

chapter 8

"Here Rottweiler, Here Rottweiler"

Thus says the Lord, "Let my people go, that they may serve me."

Exodus 8:1

Okay, it's time to get rid of this snake! He has been relaxing comfortably in our wardrobes too long. You can whistle for that Rottweiler if you want to, but the only way we can get rid of this snake is through Jesus Christ.

To understand how that is done let's go to the book of Exodus in the Old Testament. Here we read that God wanted Pharaoh, the king of Egypt, to release His children from bondage. Understand that in the Bible, King Pharaoh of Egypt represents evil and wickedness in the world. "Let my people go!" God said to King Pharaoh through His spokesman Moses. The King continued to resist the command, despite the fact that God had already sent nine plagues against the Egyptians. So God issued a last plague in order to free His people and this plague would become visible at midnight. When God's hand moved at the midnight hour, all the firstborn in the land of Egypt would die.

However, the plague was not to harm God's children. So in order for His children to be protected, God instructed them to sacrifice a lamb and place the blood on the doorposts and the lintel of their homes. In Exodus 12:13 God says, "And the blood will be a sign for you on the houses where you live; and when I see the blood I will pass over you."

What does this have to do with us today, especially with our wardrobe choices? The blood of the sacrificed lamb that protected God's people in the Old Testament was symbolic of the blood Jesus shed on the cross in the New Testament. His death was the perfect, sinless sacrifice and it broke the power of sin, protecting us today from the bondage and destruction of Satan. By the power of the shed blood of Jesus we have the authority to kick the enemy, Satan, out of our lives and our decision making (which includes decisions on clothing choices). James 4:7 says, "Submit therefore to God. Resist the devil and he will flee from you." Sounds easy, doesn't it? It is, if. . . .

Notice the first part of the scripture in James 4:7 which says, "Submit therefore to God." You're thinking, "I knew there was a catch. I'll just keep the Rottweiler for my protection, slobber and all." There is no catch, but there is a condition–you must be a child of God if you want the protection of Jesus' shed blood on the cross. God never created anyone that He did not love and because He loves us, He wants to give us the gift of love, protection, and eternal life. God wants to give us a gift and it's free! "For God so loved the world that He gave His only begotten Son (Jesus), that whosoever believes in Him should not die, but have eternal life." (John 3:16)

With this scripture in mind our responsibility is to take action if we want to be a child of

God. Our action involves three steps:

The first step is simply to understand the truth of John 3:16 and accept in faith that Jesus is the son of God, that He died for our sins, was buried and rose again on the third day and He is a living God.

The second step is to understand that it was our sins that separated us from God because God is perfect and cannot look upon sin. Romans 3:23 says, "All have sinned and fall short of the glory of God." In order to close that separation, Jesus, the perfect sacrifice, died for us so that we could be forgiven of sin and brought into fellowship with God. So as sinners we must ask God for forgiveness and desire true repentance in our hearts. Jesus said repent and believe in the Gospel (Mark 1:15).

The third step is to receive this gift in faith and we do that by talking to Jesus in the form of a prayer that can be prayed silently or aloud. Your prayer can be as simple as this: Jesus, I believe that you are the Son of God. I believe that you died on the cross for my sins. I believe that you were buried and on the third day you arose from the grave and you are a living God. Jesus, I confess my sins and I ask you to forgive me of them. I invite you to come into my heart. I accept you as Lord and Savior of my life. In Jesus' name, Amen.

If you prayed this prayer, you are in the family of God. He is your Heavenly Father. "But as many as received Him, to them He gave the right to become children of God" (John 1:12).

Also, if you prayed this prayer, you now have the power to get the snake out of your garden. Just point your finger at any temptation, past sins, hurts, fears, or anything leading you away from Godliness and say, "You Deceiver, the precious blood of Jesus is over the door of my heart and I command you to get out of my life in the name of Jesus." It works every time you apply your faith, line up your will with God's, and use the name of Jesus.

martha cahoon

chapter 9

So Now You Are a Princess

"But you are a chosen race, a royal priesthood, a holy nation, a people for God's own possession."

I Peter 2:9

How does a person get from being ordinary to extraordinary in this world? Perhaps at this point in your life your greatest expectations may be winning the lottery or the Reader's Digest sweepstakes. You just know that if you could win or qualify for something really big that it would make you somebody. This event would be the turning point in your life and give you the desires of your heart. Automatically, you will become a trendsetter and this windfall will earn you a telephone book full of new best friends.

Well, heads up! Every child of God has been awarded something better than the lottery. Our sweepstakes number is I Peter 2:9. The claim ticket has been within our reach all the while and many of us have never claimed it. It reads, "But you are a chosen race, a royal priesthood, a Holy Nation, a people for God's own possession, that you may proclaim the excellencies of Him who has called you out of darkness and into His marvelous light."

We are a "chosen people?" How did we get chosen? Was it by a popular vote or did we win a beauty contest? Were we voted the best dressed or perhaps had the best body measurements? Nope, none of these. Being a "chosen people" is part of the package deal when we accept Jesus Christ as our Savior. As the scripture says, because God loves us He makes us His royal priesthood.

Well, check it out! His royal priesthood! Yep, that's what it says on our heavenly lottery claim ticket in I Peter 2:9. Every girl has dreamed of being a princess, a part of a royal family. Now that we have accepted Jesus Christ as our Savior, that makes us the King's daughter, which makes us a princess.

Jesus has given us salvation that is free and we can do nothing to earn being chosen, but we can do something to show our responsibility in the relationship. As the scripture says, we are "God's own possession" and we are to show others how God called us out of the standards of the world into holiness. Because we are God's possession, He is going to show us how He can make us the best we can be. He will reveal to us princess possibilities like we never saw before. Undeveloped talents that have lain beneath the surface of our lives are going to be revealed and developed. Dreams we were afraid to dream can become a reality. This is possible because of what Jesus said in the last part of John 10:10, remember? "My purpose is to give life in all its fullness." (TLB)

We may be thinking, "It is going to be too hard becoming a princess, the sacrifice will be too much, the lessons too intense." Well, girlfriend, just engrave this on your princess tiara, "The things impossible with men are possible with God." (Luke 18:27). Before we were ever born, God planned His best for our lives. He knew what would satisfy us and give our lives true meaning. Now that we are a child of God, He will continually reach His hand from heaven's gates to teach us the privileges we have in Christ. These privileges are written in the Bible and it is our responsibility to seek them out, live by them, and allow God to test us on them. The more we take responsibility to love God's Word, the more we can distinguish what is of God and what is of the enemy, and the more we will be ready to receive God's best for our lives.

Let us never become careless and forget that Satan will plunder our privileges and exploit us to failure and darkness. Christ will wrap us in righteousness and exhort us to dignity and light. Every day of our lives is a lesson in becoming the righteousness of Christ.

A beautiful scripture written in Psalms 45:13 says, "The King's daughter is all glorious within. Her clothing is interwoven with gold." This is what our Father wants for His princess. Does it take your breath away to know that our Heavenly Father wants us dressed in clothing with gold? Do you notice in this scripture there are two individuals responsible for two different things? The daughter is responsible for what she will allow God to develop within her, the Father for the clothing.

Read on, Princess, and let's do our part.

chapter 10

Who is on the Best Dressed List Anyway?

"Do you not know that you are a temple of God, and that the spirit of God dwells in you?"

I Corinthians 3:16

The fashion driven world would convince us that clothing makes the woman. But if that is the case, then the well dressed mannequins in the department store windows are on the best dressed list. However, these decked out dummies are all glitz and glitter on the outside and nothing but air on the inside.

Sadly, many women in the world today

are similar to these store mannequins. We walk through life dressed according to the fashions of the world, but inside we are empty, unfulfilled, and incomplete. The next shopping binge momentarily satisfies our need for fulfillment, but that wears out before the clothing has completed its first rinse cycle in the washing machine. Perhaps we should ask God to retrain the way we view our bodies. We are not department store mannequins because we not only have an exterior, but an interior as well, and both have an appearance. I Corinthians 3:16 asks a reality check question, "Do you not know that you are a temple of God, and that the Spirit of God dwells in you?"

Fall in line behind me, girls! The realization of this truth makes me want to ride through a car wash on a skateboard while gargling with extra, extra strength mouth wash to get rid of the buildup of all the dirt inside and outside my body. "We are a temple?" "The Spirit of God lives in us?" we ask. The answer is yes–and ditto. The moment we prayed to receive Jesus as our Savior, the Holy Spirit came to live within us. To avoid being labeled a mannequin, the Holy Spirit must be given all freedom to grow and fill our temple completely. When we desire to grow in spiritual truths, the presence of the Holy Spirit will create in us wisdom, strength, and an inner beauty that does not come out of a makeup bottle or off a clothing rack. Scripture says, "Charm is deceitful and beauty is vain, but a woman that fears (loves, reveres) the Lord, she shall be praised." (Proverbs 31:30)

Continuing with I Corinthians 3:17, we read, "If any man destroys (corrupts) the temple of God, God will destroy him, for the temple of God is holy, and that is what you are." This scripture does not pull any punches. It tells the TRUTH. The temple (our body) is very precious to God and He wants it protected in every way. The truth, speaking to us in this scripture, is that if we corrupt the temple inside or out, then death can occur. There may not be blood and gore that might be seen in physical death, but we are being destroyed spiritually when we grieve the Holy Spirit (Spirit Man) within us and allow Satan (Flesh Man) to influence us. Satan has permission at this point to do his John 10:10 number on us. Remember? Kill, steal, and destroy. God makes it very clear in His Word that the temple is not for man, but for the Lord God. When we understand this truth, hopefully our desire to wear clothing "because everyone else is doing it" will come to a screeching halt. And the desire to dress the temple to glorify God will become stronger than the pressures of the world.

But we ask, "Can a woman wear beautiful, trendsetting clothing, and not be labeled as a 'Hoochie Mama'?"

To answer a question with a question, "Have you ever seen God walking in blue jeans, swimsuit, or sparkling evening wear?" I have, and each item of clothing is worn in style, beauty, and good taste and the temple is not tarnished in any way.

But we continue to stammer, "How can that be done without compromising the Holy Spirit living within us?"

When the Holy Spirit lives fully within us, He will give us the wisdom of God and we will know how to select clothing that is appropriate and in good taste. Jeans are great, just give them some slack. Bathing suits are an essential, but cover well the essential parts. Sparkling evening wear was made for a princess; just remember to reflect "The Light of the World, Jesus Christ." (John 8:12)

chapter 11

Anointed Attire

". . . . For He has clothed me with
garments of salvation, He has wrapped
me with a robe of righteousness . . ."
Isaiah 61:10

Well, now that we have thrown the Hoochie
Mama clothing out of our closets, we should
look for "anointed attire." Where do we find this
type of merchandise? Who designs this clothing? Remember in the beginning of this book the
statement was made, "The answer to all of life is
found in the Bible." Let's look there again and
find the answer.

There is a woman in the Bible who
designed the type of clothing we are looking

for. She is found in Proverbs 31 and was likely the best dressed woman around and a trendsetter in the clothing market in her world. Not only was her household clothed like royalty, but we see where "she made coverings for herself–her clothing was fine linen and purple." (Proverbs 31:22). I think it is interesting that the fabric and color of her clothing was mentioned and I believe that this is significant. The fabric is linen and because of the way fine linen is woven, it is a fabric of endurance. Interestingly, it has been a fabric that has stood the test of time and is worn by women today. The message speaking to me in this caveat is that the things of God do not go in and out of style; they are timeless and are just as alive and relevant today as they were thousands of years ago. The color of the fabric is purple and is a color of royalty and wealth. This lady may not have been royalty, but she chose purple because spiritually, she was the daughter of the King, Jehovah God, and she looked like a million dollars when she wore it. What a talented lady. I can almost visualize her as she entered a room clothed in beautiful color and fine linen cut in flattering lines.

martha cahoon

As we continue to read the scripture we see that she was so gifted in her creativity that she had a home-based business. Verse 24 of this book tells us, "She makes linen garments and sells them." I can imagine women were circling the block on their camels looking for a parking place so they could shop in her boutique.

Now here is the question. "Where is this woman today?" Have we become so sedated by the enemy that we nonchalantly accept what the world dictates as fashion? Yes, there are some good designers in the clothing industry, but there is room for many more. Keep reading and perhaps you can help me find them.

However, before we begin our search to find this clothing, I would ask you to buckle up and get focused so we can have an extreme moment at this point. There is this matter of fine linen that was mentioned in the Proverbs woman that we need to grab hold of mentally and spiritually, and to do that we have to look deeply.

So let's just camp out here a bit.

Fine Linen

The Bible is the inerrant Word of God. Its content consists of divinely woven threads of scripture of varying themes that weave themselves in and out of the pages from cover to cover. These threads serve as a tether, anchored on one end in the inerrant Word, the other end free, allowing us to explore safely as we weave through timeless writings, picking up nuggets of understanding along the way. The threads also bind together the rich history of God's people to the personal application in the present, modern day and reveal to us the absolute reality of God, His Son, Jesus Christ and the Holy Spirit.

If we search out and follow any one of these threads, and there are many, the spiritual rewards and insights are incredible. In fact, so great are the blessings of understanding that the discovery is priceless, unequaled by any human emotion. I have experienced just such a discovery as I followed the thread of *fine linen*. If my frail writing skills will allow, I will share this discovery with you. Take notice that with each sighting of my *fine linen* thread, I will follow the account with the *Spiritual Significance in Regard to Wardrobe* so that we can see the personal application to our lives today.

✎ There are close to 100 references made to *fine linen* in the Bible beginning in the first book of Genesis and finishing in the last book, Revelation. The thread first caught my attention in Genesis 41:42 where Joseph, the son of Jacob, was forced into slavery in Egypt. Joseph found himself in this predicament due to poor judgment on his part in his relationship with his brothers. None the less, over the following years of Joseph's life, he went through a number of true life adventures that would make a Harrison Ford movie look like a walk in the park. But always under the watchful eye of God, Joseph won the favor of the king of Egypt and was not only freed from slavery but was made a ruler as well. Focusing on the scripture where Joseph won favor with the king, the scripture reads, "Then Pharaoh took off his signet ring from his hand and put it on Joseph's hand and clothed him in garments of *fine linen*, and put the gold necklace around his neck." This is a victorious picture of a man once in bondage, set free and his life restored beyond anything he could imagine.

Spiritual Significance in Regard to Wardrobe: Just as Joseph was in bondage in Egypt, many women in the world today are also in bondage in any number of ways due to poor judgment in their lives. The obvious bondages are addictions (to drugs, alcohol, food, etc.), sexual promiscuity, pornography, body appearance, seductive dress, and many others. But notice that Joseph decided to live his life to reflect godliness despite his circumstances and past mistakes (you must read Genesis 41 to get the full picture, it is an awesome story). God honored his decision and against all odds performed a miracle that freed Joseph from his bondage. How? God orchestrated a series of occurrences that would bring Joseph before the Pharaoh. The Pharaoh was so impressed with Joseph and his gift of wisdom that he gave Joseph position (awarded him a signet ring), gave him freedom (dressed him in *fine linen* which was evidence of a free man), and awarded him wealth (gave him a gold necklace). When we allow God to be king in our heart, mind and soul, He sets us free from whatever binds us and He will do the same for women today that He did for Joseph centuries ago.

Of course the point that catches my attention is not the signet ring or the gold necklace but that the Pharaoh dressed Joseph in *fine linen,* which was evidence of a free man. As beneficial as wealth and position can be, they are no substitute for freedom. Only a person who has been held captive can explain the truth of this to another. You see, when we lose our freedom to make choices, many things we value in life are completely out of reach. Ask the addict whose mind and body is driven for the next fix. Ask the teenager whose life is lived by "Everybody else is doing it" and is ruled by pride and peer pressure. Ask the young mother who has kept up with the Jones' so long that her families' finances are in bondage so deep that she has lost all choices of how the budget will be spent. Apart from Christ, these circumstances are gripped tightly in bondage and freedom seems impossible. But when we put the past behind us and Christ before us, He will make a way where there seems to be no way to become free. And just as He did with Joseph, He will wrap our lives in *fine linen* which is evidence of a free woman.

This story is the beginning of many references to *fine linen* and my curiosity continues to trace this thread. I realize it is too early for you to share my excitement about this, but stay with me. I think you will be doing high fives in the end.

⌘ A second use of *fine linen* that caught my attention was in the building of the tabernacle in the Old Testament. The tabernacle was the place where God would reside among His people until later when the temple would be built. Exodus 26:1 reads, "Moreover, you shall make the tabernacle with ten curtains of fine twisted linen and blue and purple and scarlet material . . ." This example is to site just one of the many places God required linen to be used in the tabernacle. To the casual reader, this scripture may not be of any significance, but girls, you must understand how this scripture affects me. I go giddy about textiles. I love to smell them, feel them, and would even roll in them if it would not cause a scene. For me, to visualize yards and yards of linen fabrics being used throughout God's dwelling place causes me to hyperventilate with excitement. As I read these scriptures, I picture in my mind the wilderness desert and a soft breeze blowing, gently lifting the beautiful blue, purple, and scarlet linens which were held secure with clasps of solid gold. What a beautiful place this must have been for God to dwell.

Spiritual Significance in Regard to Wardrobe: Since the coming of Jesus Christ, God's plan in regard to His abiding place has far surpassed that of the tabernacle, as beautiful as it was. Through the power of the Holy Spirit, he chooses to abide in the heart of every believer and to make His home there. And just as God required minute detail as to how the Old Testament tabernacle should look, he takes the same detail with our lives today. The scripture shows that He required exact lengths and widths of the *fine linen* used in the tabernacle. I believe He also requires exact measurements in our lives as well. These exact measurements result in a linen of holiness that make up the definition of our Christian life.

As we continue through this scripture we see proof of God honoring his people for their painstaking detail preparation of the tabernacle. It is shown in one of the most extreme moments the world has ever seen. The scene reveals that everything had been completed with the building itself. The people had used their talents to do the work as well as they possibly could and they all waited, anxiously anticipating the coming of God to fill His prepared abiding place. Look to the end of this story at Exodus 40:34, 35 and the scripture reads, "Then the cloud covered the tent of meeting and the glory of the Lord filled the tabernacle. And Moses was not able to enter the tent of meeting because the cloud had settled on it, and the glory of the Lord filled the tabernacle." Can you imagine God's presence being so strong that Moses could not even get in the tabernacle and he probably had a front row seat reserved. What a breathtaking scene! All the thousands of God's people surrounded the tabernacle and they knew without a doubt, God's glory had come down! He was inside the walls made with the beautiful blue, purple and scarlet *fine linen* curtains.

Can we apply this moment to our lives? Wouldn't it be awesome that because of obedience and preparation in our lives, that the glory of the Lord would show up this powerfully in each of us? Just envision, the Father of Glory, illuminating Himself in us! To some individuals this may be a frightening thought, fear that if we allow ourselves to be so filled with God, there will be no room for the desires of our heart. Understand this ladies, God has fathered in us what He intended to give our lives fullness and Him glory, so don't short sale yourselves by second guessing the creator of the universe. He knows without doubt what is best for us. So let us purpose to continue our work, beautifully preparing in minute detail the spiritual *fine linen* curtains of our lives, weaving them with holiness, and expecting the glory of God to come down. Hallelujah! Just a taste of this concept in my life personally makes this southern girl want to shout,

martha cahoon

"I do declare, My God is in the house!" Can you imagine the impact our lives would have on those around us? Women would stop us at every turn to say, "Tell me girl friend, what makes your life so different from mine?" We would pause, take a deep breath (my witty nature likes to think that deep breath stirs those *fine linen* curtains down in our tabernacle like that desert breeze). Then put on a big Holy Spirit smile, jab one hand on a hip and tap our chest with the other hand and say, "'Cause God is in this house!" I think we would have her attention after that. This thought is so over the top that I could camp out here for a while, but we can't; my thread is on the move so let's see where it stops next.

✂ It appears my thread is lingering in the book of Leviticus where we continue to read about the tabernacle. Reading these scriptures we see that the priests who tended the tabernacle were to wear *Holy linen*. "He (the priest) shall put on the holy linen tunic and the linen under-garments shall be next to his body . . ." (Leviticus 16:4). This is only one of several accounts in the book of Leviticus showing the priest wearing

martha cahoon

linen. If you do further reading in Exodus 28, you will find there is a great fashion show on priest's apparel and it will make you stop and think before you complain about dressing up on Sunday. Pulling on a pair of pantyhose is nothing compared to the breast piece and ephod, robe, tunic, turban, and sash that the priest had to wear. And that was just a few of the items. As with the details of the linen curtains in the tabernacle, much detail was taken in the clothing and body preparations of the priests as they served in the temple (even down to their underwear).

Spiritual Significance in Regard to Wardrobe: Remember those who have accepted Jesus as their savior are a royal priesthood (I Peter 2:9). We cannot be reminded enough that God wants to dress His priests to represent and reflect Him. Not that we actually dress in linen–the actual fabric of our garment is not the issue. The issue is that godliness becomes the fabric of our lives. We, the New Testament Priests, have the same responsibility the Old Testament priests had–to be obedient and holy in our daily lives and dressed for service, wherever our ministry. What a privilege!

martha cahoon

☙ As my thread continues one cannot leave the Old Testament without again visiting the Proverbs 31 woman who inspired the search. Our eyes easily find the weaving thread . . . "Her clothing is *fine linen* and purple" (Proverbs 31:22).

Spiritual Significance in Regard to Wardrobe: God used this woman as an example to all women through the ages. However, do not get the impression that this lady was a clothes horse who wore only new fashions and they were always perfect in every way. I am sure she had mended places on her clothing that were there because of much wear and tear and hard work in her life. A godly woman does not have to wear new and expensive clothing in the latest styles to reflect holiness. Also, because a woman cannot afford new fashions does not make her any less a Proverbs 31 woman. Jesus addresses this in Matthew 6:28, 29 and 33 when He said, "And why are you anxious about clothing? Observe how the lilies of the field grow; they do not toil nor do they spin. Yet I say to you that even Solomon in all his glory did not clothe himself like one of these. But seek first His kingdom and His righteousness and all these things shall be added to you." What a wonderful promise from God. He is concerned about what His daughters wear and is willing to provide our clothing needs (not to be confused with our clothing "wants"). Also notice that since the Proverbs 31 woman was dressed in *fine linen* and purple, which is a majestic color, it is easy to see that her choice of clothing was to reflect her heavenly father. A scripture in Psalms reads, "The Lord reigns, He is clothed in majesty." (Psalms 93:1) This purple *fine linen* is an example and a goal for women's lives today, to reflect the Majesty.

Now let us leave the Old Testament and those wonderful Old Testament saints and follow the thread into the gospels of the New Testament and feel the excitement of the life and ministry of Jesus Christ. The thread moves tenderly into the book of Mark. There is an event recorded within these pages so gripping that without knowing the end of the story we would come to a paralyzing halt, unable to move any further. In chapter 15 we see the crucified body of Jesus hanging upon the cross. His body is bloody, dirty, and torn beyond recognition. A grief-stricken follower, Joseph of

Arimathea, asks the authorities for the body of Jesus to properly bury Him. The scripture reads, "And Joseph brought a *linen cloth*, took Him (Jesus) down, wrapped Him in the *linen cloth*, and laid Him in a tomb." (Mark 15:46) It appears that every hope of every individual past, present, and future was dashed in the words of this scripture. But three days later after the burial, two women came to complete the burial process for Jesus' body. To their shock and amazement, they saw an angel in the tomb and he said to them, "Do not be amazed; you are looking for Jesus the Nazarene, who has been crucified. He has risen." (Mark 16:6) The scripture clearly shows, the two women found only an empty tomb. We read the same story in the gospel of John. Three days after the burial, Simon Peter "entered the tomb and he beheld the linen wrappings lying there and the facecloth which had been on His head, not lying with the linen wrappings but rolled up in a place by itself." (John 20:6) Again, the tomb was empty except for the linen wrappings.

Spiritual Significance in Regard to Wardrobe: The scripture clearly tells us that after Jesus was buried, that on the third day He arose from the grave and all that was left behind was the borrowed linen clothing. Jesus had risen and His death had conquered every power of sin and darkness. The personal application in this scripture to believers is that when we prayed to receive Jesus as our Lord and Savior, we also are resurrected into a new life and become a new creation (2 Corinthians 5:17), leaving the old soiled things in our lives behind. There is not a woman alive that does not have old, soiled memories and experiences in her life that she desires to leave behind. Too many are all the past mistakes and condemning sins or perhaps memories of pain we have endured, that keeps coming back to embarrass and taunt us. The death of Jesus made it possible for these dirty linens to be buried in a grave of repentance in exchange for forgiveness and past sorrow to new life.

My thread comes to an end in the last book of the Bible, the book of Revelation. This book is so alive and so filled with prophesies and revelation of spiritual truths that reading the book takes much time to absorb the depth of it. But the most powerful of all the revelation words comes in Revelation 19:8, when Jesus returns for His bride, or the church, which is the believer. This scripture says, "And it was given to her (the bride) to clothe herself in *fine linen*, bright and clean, for the *fine linen* is the righteous acts of the saints."

Spiritual Significance in Regard to Wardrobe: When thought goes into it, this linen thread is obviously as big as an interstate highway. Actually it's not just big–it's huge, and Revelation 19:8 is the key to seeing the whole picture. It reads, "The bride was to clothe herself in *fine linen*, bright and clean, for the *fine linen* is righteous acts of the saints." Isn't it interesting that God used a clothing metaphor to illustrate an eternal fact that we should apply every moment of every day of our lives? The *fine linen*, bright and clean, represents the righteous acts of God's children while we are here on earth. The linen is "fine" showing that God uses His best to clothe His righteous children and notice again, it is bright and clean. As I encounter this scripture I almost sob in hopelessness, knowing my own weakness and fragile human nature. How can I possibly be righteous enough to earn *fine linen*? And even if I

martha cahoon

could, how would I stay mistake free and sinless to keep the linen "bright and clean?"

None of us are righteous; neither is our linen bright and clean. As hard as we try, we have and will again make mistakes in our lives. And yes, since we are talking about wardrobes, we may occasionally blow it with our selections as we daily present our bodies to God and to the world. Heaven forbid, there may be occasions when we stand in front of our mirrors and with one excuse or another consent to dressing our bodies with fashions that leave our belly buttons shining, cleavage bulging, thighs exposed, and pants and skirts stretched tightly over buttocks, just to mention a very few of the very obvious. We may even deceive ourselves into dressing in the borderline styles that are "perfectly accept-able" only because they are not as bad as the worst. With the Holy Spirit whispering within us, "No, no," we stand before mirrors and turn, twist, bend over, sit, and cross our legs knowing exactly which body moves will allow the gar-ment to reveal seduction. Then, after justifying the selection with thin excuses and self-righteous babble, make the deliberate decision to wear it

martha cahoon

anyway. Would a Spirit-filled Christian girl or woman actually make this mistake? Think back. Remember earlier the story about the children's choir leader? This woman had stood in front of her mirror before she left home that morning and saw what would happen when she raised her arms. She knew exactly how high the skirt would come up on her thighs and she knew it would toy with men's imaginations, yet she made the decision to wear it anyway. Like this children's choir director, when we make the choice to wear seductive clothing, we also make the choice to wear garbage outwardly on our bodies while inwardly there is the odor of filth and grime. Obviously there is no *fine linen* in the tabernacle because of compromise in our hearts and no *fine linen* outside the tabernacle because we chose to dress with seduction in mind.

"Oh, how can we ever expect to be clothed in the *fine linen*, bright and clean, that is written in Revelation 19:8 because our acts are far from righteous?"

Listen carefully, young girls and women. Our hope of wearing *fine linen* came the day our Savior, Jesus Christ, allowed His own linen garments to be stained with His precious blood as He was taken from the cross of Calvary. Not only was His linen stained with His blood, but it was made horribly filthy with the brutal, obscene, and vulgar sins of mankind that He took upon Himself. But because of Jesus' act of extreme love and obedience upon the cross, the filthy linen resulted as pure righteousness and shown forth in the eyes of God as *fine linen*, bright and clean. So today, in the lives of the *repentant* believer, Jesus supernaturally takes our daily linen, filthy from disobedience and human weaknesses, and gives to us in exchange His own *fine linen*. The Father in turn, looks through the blood of His sacrificed Son and He sees us clothed in *fine linen*, bright and clean. The love and obedience of Jesus on the cross makes that possible. Oh, hallelujah! Can we ever praise Jesus enough?

Our Heavenly Father always desires to see us in *fine linen*, so He stands ready to give us a second chance. He will never leave us without hope of forgiveness in our lives. His desire is always that we would be restored. So today, "If we confess our sins, He is faithful and righteous to forgive us our sins and to cleanse us from all unrighteousness." (I John 1:9) And may we always remember this: The Blood of Jesus that was shed was also the precious blood from the veins of God the Father. Never squander it by foolishly or deliberately making the same mistakes over and over again.

Now let us continue our search for the "Anointed Attire." By the way, I hear they are having a sale down at "Esther's Boutique." Keep reading and meet me there.

chapter 12

Esther's Boutique

"Who knows whether you have not come to the kingdom for such a time as this?"

Esther 4:14

Creativity is important to God. The first written knowledge that we have of God is in Genesis 1:1 and it says, "In the beginning God created. . . ." Can you imagine the thrill it gave our Father to create beauty for us? He must have had a big smile on His face when He dressed His first zebra with the sharp contrast of the black and white stripes on its coat. Look at the Bird of Paradise with the brilliant greens and yellows on feathers flouncing in the breezes. Also, how about the beauty of a million different flowers with colors so varied that even the skilled artist's creativity has never been able to reproduce them all.

God is the author of creativity and He has given men and women the ability to use creative talents as well. However, it appears that in the fashion industry today there are some designers who may have run out of creativity, so in order to sell their designs they have resorted to visual seduction and sensual suggestion. But we can no longer blame the designers for lack of creativity if we, daughters of the King, sit back in fear, unwilling to be challenged or motivated to use our God-given talents of creativity. There are hundreds of talented believers that whine, "It's a jungle out there! The big companies will eat us up and spit us out with all their know-how and business savvy. How can we possibly get into the clothing industry?" Then, still whining and whimpering, we struggle back to the hoochie mama clothing racks. We drag behind us our tired, old Rottweilers who are too exhausted to even slobber because they are working overtime to keep the snakes out of the designs.

martha cahoon

Remember earlier, Queen Esther was mentioned as a young woman who used good taste in dress and grooming to win a king's heart and later become his queen. Actually, she did more than win a king's heart. God used her to save His people, the Jews. In a desperate time when an evil plot was being planned to destroy the Hebrew nation, she was reminded by her godly cousin, Mordecai, about her destiny as a queen. In Esther 4:4 he says, "Who knows whether you have not come to the kingdom for such a time as this?"

Esther's countrymen were on the verge of destruction, and deliverance lay in her hands. Bravely she responded to Mordecai's challenge and after prayer and careful planning, she sprang into action. With mind set and conviction she said, "If I perish, I perish," (Esther 4:14) and she went about completing the plan God had given her, and He used her to save His chosen people.

There are many young girls and women today with the same determination and tenacity that Esther had. Combined with their strong character traits and God given talents of design and creativity, an impact can be made in the fashion world. God desires to raise up women "for such a time as this." A time when so many vulnerable women, for the sake of fashion and social acceptance, are sacrificing their bodies on the world's altar of public nudity and visual exploitation.

This creative woman of God will not fear failure or rejection or competition because greater is God who is in her than he (Satan) who is in the world. Like Esther, her heart's conviction will be, "If I perish, I perish." I cannot imagine that there would be a situation in the fashion world that would be life threatening (unless perhaps she creates a line of "drop dead" good looking fashions). However, she may risk scorn, ridicule, and rejection by many in the world. But whatever the risk, she could impact the fashion industry and make a difference in our world.

For other Godly girls and young women whose gifts may not be creativity in fashion design, you also were born "for such a time as this." Someone has to buy these new designs and make a fashion statement to the world. You play as important a part as the creative woman. When you are purchasing clothing, you will need boldness to make a statement with the styles you choose to wear or not wear. Like the woman in

Proverbs 31:25, "Strength and dignity are her clothing and she smiles at the future."

Do you realize that clothing shows strength? Webster's dictionary defines strength as, "Power to resist force or attacks." When you hear your peers saying, "You should go change clothes, girl, 'cause tonight I'm wearing my little pink thing," (which is three threads short of naked). But rather you put on your cute purple thing that is flattering and in good taste and along with the strength of the Holy Spirit within, you will not be intimidated by their "yadda yadda" and will have the strength to resist intimidation. Remember, God wants to be glorified through us and when we dress to reflect Him, He is made recognizable in us.

Proverbs 31:25 also says "dignity is your clothing." Webster defines dignity as "worth and stateliness." Incorporate these qualities into your clothing selection so that your dignity is protected. There is no dignity in a woman when all that is remembered about her is how much flesh her lack of clothing revealed. When we lovingly show others how much we are worth because of God's great gift of redemption and that our cloth-

martha cahoon

ing adorns the body in which the gift lives, we become the trendsetters because people follow confidence and stateliness.

This scripture in Proverbs concludes by saying, "And she smiles at the future." Because the Christian woman knows who she is in Christ, she faces the future in anticipation of the goodness of God. I Corinthians 2:9 says, "No eye has seen, no ear has heard, no mind has conceived what God has prepared for those who love Him." Living our lives by doing what God expects of us spiritually and not living like a Calamity Jane physically, then we can smile at the future knowing that whatever comes our way God knew it before we did and has already provided the way through it in victory.

Does this give us a new perspective on what we pull over our heads each morning? Excuses that try to justify trashy clothing on our backs are pitifully weak in light of the pain and power of the cross that was on the back of Jesus. However, the choice is ours. God gives us that liberty. Jesus died not only for our eternal salvation, but to give us the freedom to choose what is right.

Let's live in that liberty.

martha cahoon

chapter 13

Liberty

"And I will walk in liberty, for I
seek thy precepts."
Psalms 119:45

As ships sail into the New York harbor,
passengers are visually impacted by the Statue
of Liberty. This beautiful work of art has been
firmly planted for decades in this harbor repre-
senting everything that is good about American
liberty and it is displayed through this feminine
statute. Her majestic strength commands an awesome presence and to the viewing masses she
sends forth an invisible hope, though unseen, is
tangible to the senses.

I see a similarity with this statue and with

the woman that has the freedom of the Holy Spirit living within (only where the Holy Spirit lives there is immeasurable more power). Just as the Statue of Liberty sends off a presence of strength, beauty, and hope, so does the Christian woman. Her lifestyle, the choices that she makes, her visual presence and verbal impact makes a statement of strength, beauty, and hope. All of these characteristics are a result of the liberty she has found in Jesus Christ.

There is a scripture that speaks directly to the subject of liberty which says, "Now the Lord is the Spirit, and where the Spirit of the Lord is there is liberty." (II Corinthians 3:17). The simplicity of this verse applauds the application, but how does it apply to our lives personally? Here's how. As we allow the Holy Spirit to live in every area of our lives, we will find ourselves submitting more and more to God's authority. Submitting to His authority results in our obedience and our obedience becomes surrendering love. Translating this in context with our subject of wardrobe preference, we see that Christ has liberated us to have the choice to live in purity and reflect godliness. Let's live in that freedom. No longer are we in bondage to the seduction of the deceiver, Satan.

Note also, just as there are similarities between the Statue of Liberty and God's woman, there are privileges that God's woman has that the Statue does not because it is only stone and symbolism. God's woman knows that her life is not lived just by her might or power but by the Spirit of the Lord (Zechariah 4:6), causing the impossible to become possible, the weak to become strong, and the victim to become victorious.

Man has planted the Statue of Liberty in a harbor. God has planted His woman firmly by streams of water, which yields her fruit in season and her leaf does not wither and whatever she does prospers" (Psalms 1:3).

A beautiful scripture that can be coveted by every woman as a word of prophesy for her life is found in Isaiah 61:3. As I read this verse, I visualize our loving heavenly Father looking down upon us with eyes of complete love and adoration. I can just see Him turn to all of heaven as He exclaims proudly and loudly about his daughters.

" . . . a planting of the Lord for the display

of My splendor."

I pray we are precious women. I truly pray that we are a display of God's splendor, clothed in garments of salvation and wrapped in robes of righteousness.

Contact Martha Cahoon
or order more copies of this book at

TATE PUBLISHING, LLC

127 East Trade Center Terrace
Mustang, Oklahoma 73064

(888) 361 - 9473

Tate Publishing, LLC

www.tatepublishing.com